ALL RIGHTS RESERVED

CAUTION: Professionals and amateurs are hereby warned that this play is subject to royalty. It is fully protected by Original Works Publishing, and the copyright laws of the United States. All rights, including professional, amateur, motion pictures, recitation, lecturing, public reading, radio broadcasting, television, and the rights of translation into foreign languages are strictly reserved.

The performance rights to this play are controlled by Original Works Publishing and royalty arrangements and licenses must be secured well in advance of presentation. PLEASE NOTE that amateur royalty fees are set upon application in accordance with your producing circumstances. When applying for a royalty quotation and license please give us the number of performances intended, dates of production, your seating capacity and admission fee. Royalties are payable with negotiation from Original Works Publishing.

Royalty of the required amount must be paid whether the play is presented for charity or gain and whether or not admission is charged. Particular emphasis is laid on the question of amateur or professional readings, permission and terms for which must be secured from Original Works Publishing through direct contact.

Copying from this book is in whole or in part is strictly forbidden by law, and the right of performance is not transferable.

Whenever the play is produced the following notice must appear on all programs, printing, and advertising for the play:
"Produced by special arrangement with Original Works Publishing."
www.originalworksonline.com

Due authorship credit must be given on all programs, printing and advertising for the play.

Vile Affections
First Printing, 2008
Printed in U.S.A.
ISBN 978-1-934962-03-9

More Great Plays Available From OWP

Deadheading Roses
by Chris Cragin
3 Females, 1 Male

Synopsis: This play is about a rose gardener named JOHNNY who has been tragically discarded by the only man she ever loved. As she searches for healing and renewal, it is her love of nature which she rediscovers in the beauty of the desert, in her beloved animals, and finally through the earth's blessing of rain that gives her the strength to allow the inescapable and painful changes in her life to take their course. The set should be very minimal, the more that can be communicated through lights and sound the better. The location on stage shifts between a desert in Arizona, where JOHNNY and WILL lived for the first part of their marriage, a rose garden and home in Nashville, Tennessee, where they have lived since, and a small town in Arkansas, where JOHNNY was raised and where her mother still lives. Time is the present.

IceSPEAK
by Jeanette D. Farr
2 Males, 1 Female

Synopsis: Bee-Bee will do anything to be a rockstar. While walking acoss a frozen lake to meet the man who will lead her to success, she falls through the ice and struggles to survive. For the time she is trapped, she sees moments of her past, her dreams, and what may come of her life if she lives. A story asking how and why we speak, how smart we could be, and what happens when we lose it. For Bee-Bee, choosing between the one she loves and the one who will make her a star lies just beneath the surface.

VILE AFFECTIONS

by

Vanda

Acknowledgements

I began the preliminary work for VILE AFFECTIONS while sitting at a picnic table outside "The Barn" on a warm September morning during my Edward Albee Fellowship. Thank you, Edward for the opportunity to be alone with my work.

I am a member of Emerging Artists Theatre (EAT), Paul Adams, Artistic Director. EAT provided me with numerous developmental readings and a workshop production directed by Tom Wojtunik. Without this type of support finishing the play would have been very difficult.

Ultimately, VILE AFFECTIONS was produced at the New York City International Fringe Festival in August 2006. Raising money to participate in this festival was no easy matter. Luckily, I received generous support from numerous sources which I want to publicly thank. First, finding the necessary funding would not have been possible if it had not been for Karen L. Sands. Other generous folk were: The Arch and Bruce Brown Foundation, The Puffin Foundation, The faculty of Metropolitan College of New York, and Frederick and Lois Wark & Lori Wark.

I also want to thank Dixon Place and Leslie Strongwater, Artistic Associate, for producing the last scene of this play in their HOT! Festival. It was wonderful to be included with so many supportive and talented people.

I need to give a big thank you to Judith C. Brown who translated an obscure manuscript that gave us the story of Benedetta Carlini. Anyone wishing to further pursue the fascinating story of Benedetta should definitely read Dr. Brown's IMMODEST ACTS, published in 1986 by Oxford University Press. Actors preparing to play these roles will find this book especially helpful.

Playwright's Note:
A Few Words on the Historical Context of the Play

Audience members are often horrified by the play's portrayal of the nuns. It is felt that the nuns are supposed to act "more holy." I believe contemporary nuns are far more devout than nuns in centuries passed. In the Renaissance women were often forced into convents by fathers fearful of losing their fortunes to another family through marriage. During the time of this play as many as one-third to one-half of all women were housed in convents. These nuns are from the upper and the newly emerging middle class; women from the poorer classes could only become servants to the nuns.

The men in this play are genuinely upset when they witness the affair between Benedetta and Bartolomea. They do not consider hearing about two women having sex with each other sexually stimulating as a modern heterosexual man might. They are aware that heterosexual activities often occur between priests and nuns and they are also aware that homosexual activities occur between monks in monasteries, but homosexuality between nuns is difficult for their imaginations to grasp. Bartolomea's revelation is so shocking to them that they are completely at a loss as to what to say or do. The scribe who was recording the proceedings at the actual investigation had impeccable handwriting up until the lesbian sexuality was brought out. Then, Brown (1985) notes the man's penmanship became almost illegible.

The use of "material instruments" or "illicit devices (which) supplied the defects of their sex," noted Crompton in his article, "The Myth of Lesbian Impunity," was a more serious offence than that which Benedetta and Bartolomea committed. Not using "instruments" may have been what saved the women from being hanged or burned. Wearing the clothes of the opposite sex was even more serious than lesbian sex with instruments and definitely led to being burned at the stake (Remember Joan). This held true for either sex. The reasoning behind this was that cross-dressing seriously undermined the family and hence the social order. The social order (as well as obedience as stated by Caterina in Vile Affections) protected their society from dissolving into chaos. One truly disturbing punishment for both men and women was enacted in the town of Treviso (near Venice). Those who were found guilty of homosexuality had their clothes removed; they were then fastened "to a stake in the Street of the Locusts with a nail or rivet driven through" their sex organs. They remained fastened to the stake all day. The next day they would be taken outside the city to be burned.

Cast of Characters

Multi-cultural casting in all roles is strongly encouraged

BENDETTA CARLINI: passionate, dramatic, in her 20s throughout the bulk of the play. In the very beginning and in the end in her 70s.

BARTOLOMEA CRIVELLI: innocent, shy, fearful, 18 years through the bulk of the play. In the very beginning and end, in her late 60's.

FATHER PAOLO RICORDATTI: sincere, compassionate, keeping a secret from others and from himself; elderly.

PROVOST STEFANO CECCHI (pronounced Chehkee): powerful, analytical, efficient, doesn't like being challenged. 35-45 years throughout the bulk of the play, in the end in his 70s or 80s.

SISTER FIORA: gossipy, an inner sensitivity that can lead her to take vengeance when she is hurt, during the bulk of play she is in her 30s. At the very beginning and end she is in her 70s.

SISTER CATERINA: sexy, says what she thinks. During the bulk of play she is in 30s. At the very beginning and end she is in her 70s.

ANTONIO FABRICI: young, macho, run by testosterone, recent graduate of Padua University, probably not a great student.

Young Nun

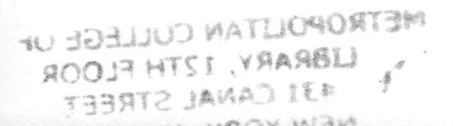

VILE AFFECTIONS by Vanda, directed by Franka Fiala, lighting by Jason Sturm was presented during the New York International Fringe Festival, August, 2006 with the following cast:

(in order of appearance)
Benedetta Carlini ....Osa Wallander
Sister Caterina..................Carol Mennie
Bartolomea......................Kate Hettesheimer
Young Nun.....................Stephanie Iannarino
Sister Fiora.....................Jacqueline Sydney
Father Paolo Ricordati........Gene Ruffini
Provost Stefano Cecchi........Scott Mitchell Kelly
Antonio Fabrici................Merrit Reid

The last scene of VILE AFFECTIONS by Vanda, directed by Rolando Ramos, lighting by Casey McLain was presented at the Dixon Place (NYC) Hot! Festival with the following cast:

(in order of appearance)
Provost Stefano Cecchi........Lennard Ridsdale
Father Paolo Ricordati.........Richard Kass
Antonio Fabrici.................Nick Fleming
Bartolomea......................Blair Baker
Benedetta Carlini...............Sara Michelle Bickweat
Caterina..........................Sandy Ziviani
Fiora..............................Selena Ambush

METROPOLITAN COLLEGE OF NY
LIBRARY, 12TH FLOOR
431 CANAL STREET
NEW YORK, NY 10013

VILE AFFECTIONS

ACT I, SCENE 1

Setting: *Sometime in July, 1660. Pescia, Italy, a short distance from Florence. The stage is dimly lit so that it has a cave-like appearance. The only set is a few rough benches, a table, a mattress, one blanket and a crucifix that hangs crookedly on the wall. The sound of women singing Gregorian chants can be heard. After a few moments an old woman wearing a black shroud with a hood that covers much of her face crawls toward the center of the stage. Her feet are bare. A moment later three old nuns, dressed in the same manner, enter. A young nun follows behind them. The palms of their hands are pressed together in prayer, the fingers pointing toward the ceiling. As they enter heading toward the table, each steps over the woman on the floor. SISTER FIORA kicks her. After stepping over the old nun on the floor they stop, turn toward the back of the stage and genuflect to the crucifix. The old woman bows her head and crosses herself. The NUNS seat themselves at the table.*

SISTER FIORA: Sisters. Bread. *(SISTER FIORA breaks off a piece of bread and passes the loaf to the other sisters. They bow their heads in a silent grace, cross themselves, eat).*

SISTER CATERINA: This all? I remember a time when we had plenty.

YOUNG NUN: When, Sister? Tell me.

FIORA: Shsh. She doesn't need to know.

CATERINA: *(To YOUNG NUN)* It was a long time ago. Before the plague, even. We don't think of it now. *(To FIORA)* But she did warn us. She told us there would be plague if we didn't listen to her.

FIORA: *(Admonishing)* Caterina.

CATERINA: Yes, Sister.

YOUNG NUN: What happened?

FIORA: It's nothing. Water under a very long bridge. You're too young to even remember the plague.

8

YOUNG NUN: But my parents told me about it. How the people of Pescia suffered.

CATERINA: Sisters. Shouldn't we, at least...? Well, just a bit of bread. Shouldn't we.... ? (*Sister Caterina nods at the old woman on the floor.*)

SISTER FIORA: I guess she best have some. (*Sister Fiora throws a piece of breads a distance away from the old woman.*) Hey, you! Catch.

(*The old woman stands to chase the bread*)

SISTER FIORA: Hey! (*FIORA snaps her fingers*)

(*The old woman looks over at FIORA, then shrinks back down to the floor. She grabs the bread and begins eating. She is ravenous, her teeth tearing into the bread as if she hadn't eaten in a very long time.*)

SISTER FIORA: Look at her, the way she eats. No more than a mere animal.

(*FIORA and the YOUNG NUN laugh and point, while the woman gnashes at the food.*)

SISTER CATERINA: When will it be enough, Fiora?

FIORA: Enough? Ask God, not me. It was not I who decreed this.

(*She continues to laugh and to encourage the YOUNG NUN to laugh by imitating the OLD WOMAN. SISTER BARTOLOMEA rises. She pours water from a pitcher into a bowl. She limps, slowly with difficulty, trying not to spill the water, toward the OLD WOMAN on the floor.*)

SISTER FIORA: Sister Bartolomea. You can't.

SISTER BARTOLOMEA: I'm not going to speak to her. I'm simply giving her a bit of water for her thirst.

SISTER CATERINA: Let me help you with that.

(SISTER BARTOLOMEA moves away from SISTER CATERINA's extended hand. CATERINA somewhat fearful does not follow. BARTOLOMEA kneels down and places the water in front of the OLD WOMAN. The OLD WOMAN grabs BARTOLOMEA's sleeve.)

OLD WOMAN: Please.

(SISTER BARTOLOMEA hesitates a moment looking into the OLD WOMAN's eyes, then gently takes the OLD WOMAN's hand from her. She returns to sit with the others. After a long moment the OLD WOMAN starts to raise herself and as she does the light grows strong. It is as if she were bringing light into that darkened room. She throws off the shroud. Underneath she wears a nun's habit and a veil upon her head. She is young. She moves toward a bench. The others pay no attention to her. She moves with great dignity and stature as if she were royalty. There is something strong and warrior-like about her. THE NUNS stand ready to leave. BARTOLOMEA watches BENEDETTA with intensity. All the NUNS except BARTOLOMEA exit. BARTOLOMEA removes the hood of the shroud to reveal a young woman dressed in a nun's habit and veil).

BARTOLOMEA: Benedetta, you won't tell, will you? There's really no need. Just confess the rest, that it's all been a lie and they won't be so terribly hard on you. *(Pause)* Benedetta?

(BARTOLOMEA waits for response. BENEDETTA stands firm, silent with a far away, trance-like look. BARTOLOMEA replaces the hood, exits as an old woman. FATHER PAOLO RICORDATI enters. He stops, standing at a distance from BENEDETTA.)

FATHER PAOLO RICORDATI: Benedetta, it's almost time. *(He pauses hoping for a response from her. There is none. She sits and goes into a deep in trance. He moves toward her, hesitantly, but still not too close.)* Benedetta? *(Pause)* Are you ready? They're at the door. Should I let them in? *(Pause, waiting)* It won't go well with you if you're like this with them. They're powerful men. The most powerful in Pescia. Men of government. *(Pause)* Please, Benedetta. *(Pause)* The Provost will have none of your moods.(Pause) I can't keep them waiting longer.*(BENEDETTA continues to look far away and beyond. FATHER PAOLO sighs and goes to the door)*. Come in, Gentlemen.

(Two men enter. FIORA, CATERINA and BARTOLOMEA, all young now, enter and standing at a distance pretend to pray. Actually they are trying to hear the words of the men.)

PROVOST STEFANO CECCHI: So that's the one, Father.

FATHER PAOLO: That is Mother Benedetta.

PROVOST STEFANO CECCHI: Mother? She's little more than a girl. And as long as this investigation goes on she is relieved of her duties as Abbess.

FATHER PAOLO RICORDATI: Is that really necessary, Stefano?

PROVOST STEFANO CECCHI: Quite. I had hoped you would've put a stop to all this nonsense years ago when it first started, Father, but I see you need me to do it. All these convents running amok nowadays. Monks and Nuns bedding each other and you Father Confessors doing nothing to stop it. Not that I care but the holy Nuncio keeps making me interrupt my own duties to investigate. And now this Benedetta Carlini. I didn't care what she was doing before. But calling down a plague on *my* town?

PROVOST and FATHER: *(Quickly crossing themselves)* May God forbid.

PROVOST STEFANO CECCHI: Oh, no. She will not.

FATHER PAOLO RICORDATI: To be fair she never said that.

PROVOST STEFANO CECCHI: She came close. Too close. There is fear under every rock and bush that the plague that rages now in Palermo will spread to us. One never knows where God's wrath might strike next. *(Quietly, eyes heavenward, as if fearful he will rouse God's wrath)* And nothing to be done about it.

FATHER PAOLO CECCHI: There is still prayer, Stefano.

PROVOST STEFANO CECCHI: *(doubtful)* Yes. *(Beat)* You remember, my Scribe, Antonio Fabrici, son of Girodano Fabrici, recent graduate of the University of Padua.

(ANTONIO and FATHER PAOLO shake hands.)

FATHER PAOLO RICORDATI: Yes. Yes, I do. Fabrici, a good old Tuscan family. You were at Benedetta's wedding.

ANTONIO: Your most humble servant, Father.

FATHER PAOLO CECCHI: *(To BENEDETTA. Almost afraid to disturb her)* Benedetta, this is Provost Cecchi who has come to...

PROVOST STEFANO CECCHI: Girl, do you know what this investigation is about?

(BENEDETTA continues her meditation.)

PROVOST STEFANO CECCHI: Do you know how serious this is? Well?! *(Beat)* Very well. Antonio read out the charge.

ANTONIO: Yes, sire. *(Antonio takes out a rolled piece of paper and unrolls it)* Benedetta Carlini, you have been charged with the crime of false mysticism. You are to be investigated for said crime by Stefano Cecchi, Provost of Pescia. If you are found guilty, depending on the cause, you will suffer the punishment of life imprisonment or death by burning. This has been so ordered by the holy Nuncio, Alfonso Giglioli.

PROVOST STEFANO CECCHI: *Now*, do you understand the seriousness of this investigation?

(BENEDETTA continues her meditation)

FATHER PAOLO RICORDATI: Benedetta, you must answer the Provost when he speaks to you. *(To PROVOST)* She doesn't mean anything by these silences.

PROVOST STEFANO CECCHI: *(To BENEDETTA)* I've come to examine you. Stand.

(BENEDETTA continues her meditation.)

PROVOST STEFANO CECCHI: I said stand and let yourself be examined. *(Beat)* Very well. If that is how it must be. *(The PROVOST nods at Antonio, who comes over.)*

ANTONIO: Sire? *(The PROVOST gestures toward BENEDETTA and ANTONIO understands. ANTONIO grabs BENEDETTA from behind and with his hands on her breasts he pulls her to her feet.)* She has a nice feel to her.

PROVOST STEFANO CECCHI: Mind where you put your hands, Antonio.

ANTONIO: Oh. Sorry, sire.

FATHER PAOLO RICORDATI: Stefano, surely this treatment isn't necessary. Let me talk to her and...

PROVOST STEFANO CECCHI: You have had eight years to 'talk' to this woman. And yet you have accomplished nothing. *(PROVOST grabs BENEDETTA's hand. HE studies it, then the next one)* Bring me a bowl of water and a towel.

(FATHER PAOLO signals to the NUNS. CATERINA goes for water and towels. THE PROVOST leans over BENEDETTA studying her feet. FATHER PAOLO stands near by like a concerned protector.)

BENEDETTA: Is it not as our Lord Jesus said it would be?

PROVOST STEFANO CECCHI: *(To all)* She speaks. *(To BENEDETTA)* Quiet!

ANTONIO: Do you see anything, Monsignor? The people in town say she's quite a wonder and they're afraid if you alienate her she'll release a horrible plague.

(The MEN hurriedly cross themselves)

ANTONIO: May God forbid. And they say....

PROVOST STEFANO CECCHI: Silence! Stop prattling on. I am well acquainted with what she said. Why do you think I am here?

(CATERINA lays the towels and bowl of water near PROVOST and retreats. The PROVOST wipes one of BENEDETTA's feet with water and a towel. He shows the towel to ANTONIO.)

PROVOST STEFANO CECCHI: What does that look like to you?

ANTONIO: I'm not sure. It does look a little red, doesn't it?

PROVOST STEFANO CECCHI: *(To BENEDETTA)* Take off your veil. Let me see your forehead.

(She looks to FATHER PAOLO for direction)

FATHER PAOLO RICORDATI: She cannot! It is a shame for a nun to appear in public with her head uncovered.

PROVOST STEFANO CECCHI: This is not public.

FATHER PAOLO RICORDATI: Please Stefano, remember yourself and your lessons as a boy at my knee.

PROVOST STEFANO CECCHI: A lifetime ago, Father, but very well. Move your veil back from your forehead only a little. So I may see. Surely, no one can object to that.

(PROVOST looks directly at FATHER PAOLO as if daring him. FATHER PAOLO nods his ascent. The PROVOST pokes at her forehead. She winces. He runs the towel across her forehead. HE stares at the towel in his hand, shows the towel to ANTONIO.)

PROVOST STEFANO CECCHI: Well?

ANTONIO: It could be blood, sire. It *is* red.

PROVOST STEFANO CECCHI: It's dry and scaly. It's hard to tell, but it could be. *(To BENEDETTA)* How did these marks come to be on your body?

BENEDETTA: *(As she speaks she becomes gradually more dramatic, possessing center stage)* Jesus, our Lord God, came to my cell while I lay abed and all the house and town slept. His body, wounded, pierced by a star, he moved toward me. The rays of that star glowed in Him. It illumined my room, setting it ablaze with a mighty fire. And through that fire our Lord appeared, coming to me as the bridegroom comes, filled with a burning compassion. And the fire ripped through my hands and feet as he blessed me with his very own holy wounds and I was brought upward into his breast as I...

PROVOST STEFANO CECCHI: How many rays were on the star?

BENEDETTA: What?

PROVOST STEFANO CECCHI: Rays? How many were there? Come, come. *(To ANTONIO)* Get this down.

ANTONIO: Yes, sire.

BENEDETTA: (Guessing) Five?

PROVOST STEFANO CECCHI: What color was the Lord's gown?

BENEDETTA: Color?

PROVOST STEFANO CECCHI: Yes, color! What color? If the Lord truly appeared to you, you must have seen the color of his gown.

BENEDETTA: But it wasn't like that. It wasn't like numbers and colors of gowns. It was a sense of...

PROVOST STEFANO CECCHI: Were you lying down or sitting up when he arrived?

BENEDETTA: I was asleep. Until he woke me. In a blaze of light the heavens opened. My legs became parted one from the other as I, too, was opening. Opening as the morning glory's petals open to greet the new day. Opening as Mother Mary was open to receive. I became that open vessel and was opened by He who has no sunset. I was opening to all that...

PROVOST STEFANO CECCHI: How long did he stay?

BENEDETTA: *(Trying to contain her irritation at his foolish question)* A little longer than never, a little shorter than forever.

ANTONIO: How do I write that down, sire?

PROVOST STEFANO CECCHI: Skip it for now. It seems our would-be mystic is playing with us. You best watch yourself, girl.

PROVOST STEFANO CECCHI: How were your feet placed? Beside each other?

BENEDETTA: No. They were on top of each other much in the manner of our Lord during His passion, but I do not remember how they got that way.

PROVOST STEFANO CECCHI: Ah! But just before you said they were parted.

BENEDETTA: *After* they were parted they were on top of each other.

PROVOST STEFANO CECCHI: I see *(Beat)* Are you in pain from those markings?

BENEDETTA: I have no pain on Sundays, Mondays and Tuesdays, but I have much pain on the other days. Fridays are the worst.

PROVOST STEFANO CECCHI: I see. Then today being Monday you are not in pain.

BENEDETTA: No, Monsignor.

PROVOST STEFANO CECCHI: Good. Good. And your side. Is it similarly affected?

BENEDETTA: Yes, Monsignor.

PROVOST STEFANO CECCHI: Open your tunic. I will examine it.

FATHER PAOLO RICORDATI: Stefano, I must object. The rules of modesty forbid it.

PROVOST STEFANO CECCHI: This woman has been claiming to get messages from Jesus and his angels, working up the whole town for years. We must be allowed to investigate the evidence. Open your tunic.

(BENEDETTA, demurely, turns her back to the audience and opens her tunic. Only the PROVOST moves to look at her side.)

FATHER PAOLO RICORDATI: *(Very uncomfortable)* You won't be long, Stefano. Don't take too long with that.

(BENEDETTA opens her tunic more. ANTONIO tries to sneak a peak, but a look from the PROVOST stops him from proceeding)

ANTONIO: Pardon, Monsignor.

(The PROVOST gets the bowl and towel. HE dips the towel in, rubs BENEDETTA's side roughly. She moans in pain.)

FATHER PAOLO RICORDATI: Stefano, be careful!

(The PROVOST looks at the towel. ANTONIO moves to look.)

ANTONIO: Blood.

PROVOST STEFANO CECCHI: Mother, close your tunic.

BENEDETTA: Did you expect it to be otherwise when the Son of God, Himself, has proclaimed it to be so?

PROVOST STEFANO CECCHI: Silence! *I* will ask the questions. When was your first vision?

(BENEDETTA has gone back into a trance.)

PROVOST STEFANO CECCHI: How can she be like this? Does she not know who I am? The power I have?

BENEDETTA *(From a deep meditative place)* You have no more power than Christ has given you.

(The PROVOST slaps her across the face.)

FATHER PAOLO RICORDATI: Stefano!

PROVOST STEFANO CECCHI: Just as surely as the earth is planted firmly in the center of this universe and the sun revolves around it you will cooperate with this investigation, girl.

BENEDETTA: *(Unflinching)* It was during morning prayers.

(BENEDETTA joins The NUNS as the sound of morning prayers being sung is heard in the background. The men retreat to the side.)

NUNS: *(In unison)* Hail Mary, Full of Grace, the Lord is with Thee. Blessed art Thou among women and blessed is the fruit of Thy womb, Jesus. Holy Mary, Mother of God pray for us sinners now and at the hour of our death. Hail Mary, Full of Grace, the Lord is with Thee. Blessed art Thou among women and blessed is the fruit of Thy womb, Jesus.

(BENEDETTA stops saying the prayer as she seems to see something. She steps away from the group and stares upward. The other women look at each other as they continue the prayer. Joy and ecstasy overtakes BENEDETTA's face.)

BENEDETTA: Lord.

(The other women stop praying and watch. BENEDETTA slowly moves to her knees, never taking her eyes and ears off the something that is there for her.)

BENEDETTA: Jesus. Jesus, yes. *(With arms outstretched, reaching upward)* Jesus. Take me. I am wholly and completely yours.

(She collapses face forward with her arms outstretched like she was nailed to a cross. All the NUNS except BARTOLOMEA kneel, cross themselves, fearful of going too close. There is a gradual changing of the lights as BARTOLOMEA approaches BENEDETTA's prostrate body).

BARTOLOMEA: Benedetta? *(beat)* Benedetta are you still with us?

PROVOST STEFANO CECCHI: *(To BARTOLOMEA)* How often did you witness something like this?

BARTOLOMEA: Many times, Provost.

PROVOST STEFANO CECCHI: And how long did she stay like that, generally speaking?

BARTOLOMEA: Hours or days. Sometimes she would appear to be merely sleeping and other times she seemed to be quite awake, but only staring. Like she could see you, but she also couldn't. I think it was those times that her spirit walked with Jesus and his angels.

PROVOST STEFANO CECCHI: Well, rouse her now. I have more questions.

BARTOLOMEA: I cannot, Monsignor. Only Jesus can say when she will return to us.

PROVOST STEFANO CECCHI: Benedetta, get up. Get up, I tell you! (*BENEDETTA does not move*) Father, can't *you* do something?

FATHER PAOLO RICORDATI: I'm sorry, Stefano.

PROVOST STEFANO CECCHI: Sorry? You're sorry? I am a busy man and the church has charged me with...(*BENEDETTA begins to writhe on the floor and make strange sounds. Her body whips in and out and knocks into the PROVOST's legs. He jumps back*). What's wrong with her? Is she ill?

BARTOLOMEA: She makes the writhing movements of the Saints of yore.

PROVOST STEFANO CECCHI: Well, make her stop it.

BARTOLOMEA: I cannot.

PROVOST STEFANO CECCHI: (*BENEDETTA's body continues to thrash as she makes odd, almost animal-like sounds. She keeps bumping into the PROVOST. He hops up and down trying to avoid her, but she keeps knocking into him.*) Do something! Somebody help! Make her stop! She's mad! She's a witch! A witch! Don't come near me, witch, demon!

(*ANTONIO moves out of her way, also frightened, but he keeps writing in his book. FATHER PAOLO and the NUNS, calmly watch the scene. They've seen this before.*).

PROVOST STEFANO CECCHI: (*The PROVOST jumps onto a chair, looking like a woman afraid of a mouse*) Lord, help me! Help me.

(*BENEDETTA's body gradually slows its movement until she lies quietly. The PROVOST gets down from the chair and cautiously approaches her, trying not to look as fearful as he feels.*)

PROVOST STEFANO CECCHI: She's a witch.

(BENEDETTA *slowly rises. Everyone watches. As she moves to leave everyone parts to let her pass. She exits with serenity.*)

PROVOST STEFANO CECCHI: (*After a moment*) Antonio, did you get all that down? What that little witch did?

ANTONIO: Yes, Monsignor.

FATHER PAOLO RICORDATI: Even the part where Benedetta made the Monsignor hop about like a little girl?

PROVOST STEFANO CECCHI: Let me see that. (*The PROVOST snatches the notebook from ANTONIO's hand and tears a page from the book, throws it away*) Careful, Father. I have the power to keep your girl locked up where she will never have any influence over my town.

FATHER PAOLO RICORDATI: Perhaps that would be for the best.

(*The lights change. BENEDETTA enters*)

BENEDETTA: Father Confessor, how can you say that?

(*Lights focus on FATHER PAOLO and BENEDETTA*).

FATHER PAOLO RICORDATI: Benedetta, we must be certain that your visions are not from the devil. You must put them to a test. Only to be sure they are from God. Remember the devil and his demons make a pleasing presence so that they might capture the devout. Women are most vulnerable to the devil because they are weak so you must be careful.

PROVOST STEFANO CECCHI: What did she say to that?

BENEDETTA: (*To FATHER PAOLO*) I will do whatever you would have me do. You are my Father Confessor sent to me by Christ. He has taught me that obedience is the most important virtue. What must I do?

FATHER PAOLO RICORDATI: Pray that God send you travails and much pain. Not ecstasies. Though this may seem harsh it will prove your visions are from He who loves us wisely and not from the trickster.

BENEDETTA: Yes, Father, if you think this is best.

FATHER PAOLO RICORDATI: And when the spirit comes to you snap your fingers in its face like this *(He demonstrates.)* That will make any demon hesitate to possess your soul.

BENEDETTA: Yes, Father.

FATHER PAOLO RICORDATI: Remember, Benedetta. Like this. *(He demonstrates again and exits.)*

BENEDETTA: *(BENEDETTA kneels)* Oh, Father of Heavenly Hosts, look down upon me, your lowly servant and bless me with pain and agony. Domine Iesu, dimitte mobis debita nostra, salva nos ab igne inferiori, perduc in caelum animas, praesertim eas, quae misericordiae tuae maxime indigent. Oh my Jesus forgive us of our sins. Save us from the fires of hell. Lead souls into heaven, especially those in most need of thy mercy. Domine Iesu, dimitte.... *(As she prays, the lights grow dim. BENEDETTA sees something or someone. She addresses it.)* No. You must not touch me. I belong to Christ. *(She backs away).* No. You mustn't do this. *(She snaps her fingers at the "thing" that she sees)* I have no desire, but for Christ. *(The "thing" keeps coming at her, she keeps snapping at it and backing up. The "thing" starts to caress her body.)* No, please, you mustn't. I can resist you. I can. You mustn't do this. I belong only to Christ. *(She writhes against the caresses of the thing, but at times it appears that her body may give into the pleasure this "thing" gives. Her breathing becomes labored as she struggles with her own desires)* No, you are not Him. Don't do this. You are not my beloved Jesus. Don't—don't make me. I will not do this sin. *(Her arms and legs are thrown open as if she were tied spread eagled. She is growing more helpless against the sexual feelings this "thing" is making her feel).* I WILL NOT DO THIS SIN! IN—IN THE NAME OF, THE NAME OF THE FATHER-- THE FATHER, THE SON, THE, THE—HOLY GHOST. *(She collapses onto the floor. The demon is gone.)*

(THE NUNS run in, holding candles. The lights get brighter as they enter.)

21

FIORA: Benedetta! Benedetta, wake yourself! What has happened?

BENEDETTA: Oh, dear Sisters. The most terrible of visions and torments. Satan, himself, sent his demon to kill me.

FIORA: Oh, dear! And what did this demon look like? Did he have horns and a tail as we have been told?

BENEDETTA: No, dear Fiora, he came in human form. He was quite beautiful. That is how Satan tempts us.

CATERINA: What did he do to you?

FIORA: *(Hungry for gossip)* Yes. Tell us.

BENEDETTA: Well-- first, he beat me. With his fists he beat me.

(The WOMEN gasp, totally involved in her story)

FIORA: How did you bear it?

BENEDETTA: I prayed to God. But that made this devil angrier, but instead of beating me more, he touched me in the forbidden places. I felt such horrible pain I thought I would go out of my mind. But that was not the worst of it.

FIORA: What was the worst? Hurry, Benedetta don't keep us waiting.

BENEDETTA: He.... I blush to think of it. No. I cannot say it aloud.

BARTOLOMEA: But Benedetta, you must. Please. Tell us.

BENEDETTA: *You* want to know?

BARTOLOMEA: (*BARTOLOMEA shyly lowers HER eyes away embarrassed by BENEDETTA's look.*) Yes. Very much.

BENEDETTA: Well, then-- if it is to be for you, little bird, I think I can find my courage.

FIORA: Then, hurry! Before the cock crows and all the house is up and snooping into our business. We must be first to know. What did he do to you, Benedetta?

BENEDETTA: He...

FIORA: Yes?! Yes?!

BENEDETTA: .. attempted to...

CATERINA: For God's wounds, woman, tell us!

BENEDETTA: to know me.

(BARTOLOMEA and FIORA gasp)

FIORA: But you didn't...?

BENEDETTA: I resisted him, of course.

FIORA: Of course.

CATERINA: Well, for God's blood, why?

FIORA: Caterina!

BENEDETTA: I belong to Our Lord. I would never betray Him.

CATERINA: You woke me up for this? I'm going to bed.

(CATERINA exits.)

FIORA: Never mind her. You suffered greatly and did well to resist. What if he returns?

BENEDETTA: He will. He wants my soul. Fiora, as the eldest, you must help me. I need a companion who will stay with me at all times. To keep watch over my soul so that it is not snatched away from me while I sleep, or reel the silk. Now, if Bartolomea...

BARTOLOMEA: What?!

FIORA: Yes. Of course. She's the youngest and therefore the

strongest. *(Turning to Bartolomea)* Bartolomea....

BARTOLOMEA: Me?! She's talking demons and devils!
FIORA: And I'll kick you from pillar to post if you refuse. You do know the stories they tell of me.

BARTOLOMEA: *(Quietly)* Yes.

FIORA: Then, you'll sleep here from now on, taking care of our blessed Benedetta. Good night, Sisters. (*FIORA exits.*)

BENEDETTA: *(BENEDETTA takes out a blanket)* Lie down. I'll cover you.

BARTOLOMEA: Is it true what they say about her?

BENEDETTA: You mean that she stabbed a young novice in the heart with a pair of scissors?

BARTOLOMEA: *(Beat)* Yes.

BENEDETTA: *(Getting into bed)* Nothing could be proved against her, but, yes, I do believe it's true. Good night. (*BENEDETTA pulls the blanket over HER own shoulders and blows out the candle.*)

(*The room grows dark. BENEDETTA goes to sleep. BARTOLOMEA remains awake, wide-eyed and very alert. After a few moments of silence, there is a scream (BENEDETTA's). BARTOLOMEA's weaker scream follows. BARTOLOMEA lights a candle holding it up to see.*)

BENEDETTA: *(Speaking to a vision)* My Lord. I did not know it was you.

BARTOLOMEA: What? Where? Where Benedetta? Where?

BENEDETTA: Oh, Lord, Lord, I am not worthy that you should come to me. Surely, there are others far more deserving.

(*BARTOLOMEA kneels and crosses herself. The lights come up on the PROVOST, ANTONIO and FATHER PAOLO.*)

PROVOST STEFANO CECCHI: *(To BARTOLOMEA)* Well, did you see anything?

BARTOLOMEA: Yes. Yes, I did, Monsignor. Benedetta placed her body in the form of Christ on the cross.

(BENEDETTA in an ecstasy arranges her body according to BARTOLOMEA's testimony.)

BENEDETTA: As You will have me, Lord.

BARTOLOMEA: And as she did so, she cried out.

BENEDETTA: But, Lord, Lord, choose another. I am but a lowly sinner. I deserve only to serve you as your humblest of servants, as the dust beneath your poorest peasants' feet. But let it not be as I will. Oh, Lord. Thy will be done with me. *(Her body goes rigid while staying in the crucified pose. She speaks in a rising crescendo.)* Lord! I feel you. I feel you deep within me. Oh, oh, you are inside me. You hum through me like a thousand singing stars. I love you. I love you. I love you. I live only to love you more. *(She screams and breathes heavily and screams again and it is the rising scream of approaching orgasm. It continues through BATOLOMEA's next words.)*

BARTOLOMEA: And then-- and then, Monsignor Provost, Father Paolo, the bed shook and Benedetta's body arched and she called out again.

BENEDETTA: *(The highest point of the orgasm)* Lord! Yes!

BARTOLOMEA: Benedetta, what is it?

BENEDETTA: *(Weak from her experience)* Bartolomea, take my hand.

BARTOLOMEA: *(As she takes BENEDETTA's hand she speaks to the PROVOST.)* I brought her hand close to my face and in the weak light of a candle I saw it. A red spot that had not been there before. I hurried to look at the other hand.

BARTOLOMEA: *(She does this)* And it, too, had the same red spot. *(She scurries down the bed to BENEDETTA's feet)* And the feet. The same.

PROVOST STEFANO CECCHI: And the side?

BARTOLOMEA: *(Embarrassed)* The side? Oh, Monsignor, I couldn't, uh....

FATHER PAOLO RICORDATI: Stefano, you know this girl could not break the rule of modesty to...

BENEDETTA: *(Impassioned)* Oh, Lord, what are you doing to me? *(She jumps from her bed. She is soaked in blood. It is dripping down her face, her arms, but the largest concentration of blood is on the lower part of her tunic, like the blood of menstruation. The men, repelled, back away.)* The blood. The blood. It pours from me like a fountain. I cannot see. It is too thick. Oh, Lord, the blood spews forth from me, from hands and feet and body. My tunic sticky with blood; it clings to me. Oh, Lord, what is this? *(She runs toward the MEN who back further away.)* Is this not enough for you? Is it not enough?

CATERINA: Towels. Bring towels. Fiora, Bartolomea hurry.

(FIORA rushes in with towels. BARTOLOMEA kneels and crosses herself but does not approach.)

FIORA: Here, Caterina.

FATHER PAOLO RICORDATI: *(From a distance, afraid to move closer)* Do you need my help? Oh, I see you don't.

(CATERINA and FIORA blot at the blood.)

PROVOST STEFANO CECCHI: *(To the other men)* The blood, there's so much of it. What could cause so much blood?

ANTONIO: Only God. *(ANTONIO kneels, but not too close to BENEDETTA, crossing himself.)*

PROVOST STEFANO CECCHI: Father, what say you?

FATHER PAOLO RICORDATI: Has not God's voice spoken in the center of this investigation and brought a miracle to guide us?

PROVOST STEFANO CECCHI: Then, you *do* believe that she...

FATHER PAOLO: She teaches nothing against church doctrine.

PROVOST STEFANO CECCHI: Antonio pick up those towels and take them out.

ANTONIO: But that's for women to do.

PROVOST STEFANO CECCHI: Do it!

ANTONIO: Yes, sire. *(With a look of disgust ANTONIO picks up the towels.)*

(FIORA and BARTOLOMEA help BENEDETTA off.)

CATERINA: *(As ANTONIO exits he pinches CATERINA in the rear. She slaps him in the behind.)* You watch yourself, little one. You're way over your head.

ANTONIO: And *you're* no Snow Maiden. *(ANTONIO dashes off.)*

(CATERINA exits with the other nuns.)

PROVOST STEFANO CECCHI: I wasn't asking you about Church Doctrine and you know it. Do you think she's an actual visionary living in our midst? In little Pescia?

FATHER PAOLO RICORDATI: I cannot help you, Stefano. God has appointed you to this. You must decide for yourself.

PROVOST STEFANO CECCHI: Dammit! That's what all you church fellows say! The Nuncio leaves it up to me to decide. But what do I know of these godly matters. But I must decide because you religious will not. You have already made too many mistakes. So now you want out of it and yet you will not let go of it. Instead, you place this burden on my shoulders and if I decide wrongly it is *I* who will be brought down while you are all tucked safely behind your cathedral walls. *(Pause)* I find no real fault in her and yet... If I tell the people, that, yes, she is from Jesus, if I recommend that she be allowed to continue what happens if later it becomes clear that she is a fraud or worse, from the devil. I will look the fool to my own town, my family name will be disgraced. Maybe the Office of the Inquisition will even find me complicit in her crimes. But if I decide against her and it turns out she *is* sent from Jesus--- then what-- what, dear pastor, will become of my soul?

FATHER PAOLO RICORDATI: Is that what concerns you, Stefano? The destiny of your soul?

PROVOST STEFANO CECCHI: *(Pause)* Bartolomea Crivelli!

BARTOLOMEA: (*Hesitantly entering.*) Yes, Sire?

PROVOST STEFANO CECCHI: I am not finished with you yet. You testified that you witnessed Benedetta receive the stigmata from Our Lord. What happened after that?

BARTOLOMEA: Happened? Uh, uh... Oh! I remember.

(*The other NUNS scurry in.*)

BARTOLOMEA: *(To other nuns)* And I was there when Christ came. Oh, such a frightsome, glorious sight.

FIORA: What did Jesus look like?

CATERINA: Yes. Was he handsome? I bet he was.

(*Benedetta enters. The other nuns drop to their knees and cross themselves.*).

BENEDETTA: Oh, Sisters, please. Don't put me above yourselves. I am come to serve, not to be served. Please. Rise. *(They do.)* It is I who should kneel before you. *(She kneels.)*

BARTOLOMEA: *(Very upset)* No! *You* kneel to me? No, Benedetta rise. You must not prostrate yourself to me. Never, never, never...

BENEDETTA: (*BENEDETTA rises.*) Peace, Little Sister. Your wisdom has made it clear. We, Sisters, must all be equals. Equals in the Lord's work.

CATERINA: Benedetta, I was wondering. Could I sit next to you tonight at supper? I'd like to ask you a favor.

FIORA: Why you? What do you care about miracles? You're going to hell anyway. I know which monk you've been "fraternizing" with.

CATERINA: Me? What about you and that poor novice you buried under the....

FIORA: Shut up if you don't want to end up lying next to her.

BENEDETTA: Sisters, sisters, please. We must keep peace with each other. *(FIORA and CATERINA bow their heads and put their hands in prayer position. BENEDETTA addresses BARTOLOMEA.)* You, little lost bird, you shall sit next to me tonight at supper.

BARTOLOMEA: *(Pleased and proud)* Me? You want me?

FIORA: But you have two sides! Surely, I'm worthy enough for your other side. I need to speak to you about, well-- maybe you could speak to Our Lord on my behalf about cutting down my time in purgatory?

CATERINA: But I was going to ask her that.

FIORA: You?! Hah!

BENEDETTA: Sisters, please, no more fighting. We must attend to our prayers and purify ourselves from impure thoughts.

CATERINA: I always have trouble with that one. *(Crosses herself)*

BENEDETTA: And we must discipline ourselves well.

FIORA: Sisters! We must elect Benedetta Carlini as our Mother Abbess. Then good favors will fall upon our house from the heavens above and people will come from miles around to buy our silk.

CATERINA: You've got my vote Benedetta.

BENEDETTA: Oh, dear, Sisters, I don't know. To take office would raise me above you, when I should be counted least of all.

BARTOLOMEA: Benedetta, won't you please be our leader. I'd feel so much safer.

BENEDETTA: Would you? *(BARTLOMEA smiles shyly. BENEDETTA addresses the group)* Well, then, if my puny self can be of service to you I cannot refuse.

FIORA: Here Benedetta. You must wear the cloak of your position. *(She takes out a cloak and puts it lovingly around BENEDETTA's shoulders)*

BENEDETTA: Bless you, dear Fiora. To our labors, Sisters. *(To CATERINA, putting an arm around her)* Caterina, perhaps, I can be of some help to you with your problem. We must pray together.

CATERINA: Oh, yes, Benedetta, yes. Thank you.

(They leave arm-in-arm.)

FIORA: *(FIORA watches them. Speaks to herself)* Well, will you look at those two? And what about *my* problems, dear Mother Carlini?

(They all exit except BARTOLOMEA.)

PROVOST STEFANO CECCHI: Then what happened? I am too important a man to be listening to this female foolishness. Let's get to something I can use. Do you not understand that we must discover the truth or we shall be lost?

FATHER PAOLO RICORDATI: We, Paolo?

PROVOST STEFANO CECCHI: *(Pause)* Go on, Sister. Go on.

(BENEDETTA, in her Abbess cloak, sits at her desk reading mail and writing in a book. The other Nuns in a different room sit talking while they embroider or knit.)

CATERINA: So exciting. Having a mystic as our very own Abbess.

FIORA: Do you really believe she *is* a mystic?

BARTOLOMEA: Yes! And someday she will be as great as Teresa of Avila or, or St Catherine of Siena even. She's my favorite. And Benedetta's too.

FIORA: Did you hear she's her father's only daughter and yet he brought her here? He never even *tried* to get her a good husband and I hear he could've afforded it.

CATERINA: Well *your* father brought you here too.

FIORA: But *I* wasn't the only daughter. Too many sisters, too many dowries. *(Pause)* I was the last. Seven sisters before me. My brothers long ago situated in good marriages. My mother dead at 33 years. Giving me life. Oh, but my father never blamed me. It broke his heart when there was so little dowry left for me. He didn't say that. But I knew. He loved me. He did. *(Pause)* Well. Most have gone on to Jesus now anyway. The plague. *(They all quietly cross themselves.)* So I suppose none of it matters any more.

CATERINA: I'm sorry, Fiora. Truly.

FIORA: Oh, pff. It's nothing.

CATERINA: It was so different for me I forget not everyone wanted this. I ran here. As soon as my husband died, may the devil keep him, I was at the door, begging to be let in.

FIORA: Heavens, whatever for?

CATERINA: Because here I am free. I have my little cell and my plays to write and mostly I'm left alone to discover the sounds and colors that lie beyond my window. Oh, there are some rules to follow, but I have no man to rule my life at his whim and that suits me well. And I like to hear the singing of the prayers. Sometimes in the early morning hours when we sing Vespers, I stop singing and listen. I listen to the sound of women singing. It is then when I am sure that we are truly about a holy endeavor here. I wish I were still a virgin.

FIORA: What?! You're the one who always has ants in her pants.

BARTOLOMEA: *(Embarrassed)* Oh, please, don't talk that way.

CATERINA: I never said I wasn't easily tempted. Oh, temptation, you wicked girl! You come to trap me with that devil cock. But the virgin is holy, peaceful, I think. And God loves them best. They bless everyone whom they pass by. Like Benedetta.

FIORA: Well, she's not the only virgin around here.

BARTOLOMEA: But she's the holiest one. Jesus chose her for himself.

FIORA: Why would Jesus choose her? I mean really. Think about it. A girl from the mountains at the poorest convent in Pescia?

BARTOLOMEA: *(Upset)* But, someday, it's gonna be the best one. Benedetta's gonna make it best. It's gonna be best in the whole world! *(She runs out.)*

FIORA: Well, what on earth got under *her* tail feathers?

CATERINA: She looks up to Benedetta. You have to remember she's young.

FIORA: I was only talking.

CATERINA: You talk too much.

(BARTOLOMEA runs past BENEDETTA.)

BENEDETTA: Bartolomea, where are you going in such a rush? The Lord bids us move slowly and deliberately, always meditating on He who gives us life.

BARTOLOMEA: I'm sorry, but that Fiora makes me so mad.

BENEDETTA: And the Lord bids we forgive, especially those who are most difficult to forgive. Now, I want to discuss some budgeting issues with you.

BARTOLOMEA: With me?!

BENEDETTA: Certainly. You're capable. Let's look over this book here. In this column we keep records of how much dowry money has been collected from the new girls coming in and over here we list how many scudos each cell costs and here...

BARTOLOMEA: Numbers, numbers! Everywhere numbers! Benedetta, please!

BENEDETTA: Why so upset?

BARTOLOMEA: You expect too much of me. You think I can do that. I can't even read.

BENEDETTA: I see. (Beat) We must do something about that. How can I have an assistant who cannot read?

BARTOLOMEA: Assistant? Me?

BENEDETTA: If you want to be.

BARTOLOMEA: Oh, yes, yes, Benedetta.

BENEDETTA: Then we must begin your lessons. Today. Now. Come. Sit.

BARTOLOMEA: Me? There? In *your* chair?

BENEDETTA: In *my* chair. (*BARTOLOMEA hesitantly sits in BENEDETTA's chair. BENEDETTA places a book in front of her.*)

PROVOST STEFANO CECCHI: No, no, no! What is this? Gossip and reading lessons? What shall I do with this?

(*A bell chimes.*)

FATHER PAOLO RICORDATI: Stefano, the hour grows late and soon there shall be no more sun. It is time for evening mass. Join us. You and your man. It will refresh your soul for tomorrow's questions.

(*There is the sound of NUNS chanting off stage.*)

ANTONIO: Let's stay, sire.

PROVOST STEFANO CECCHI: I don't know. Mass here? With that woman? What will the town think?

FATHER PAOLO RICORDATI: They will think you are doing a thorough and fair investigation, Provost Cecchi. As fair as the man that you are.

PROVOST STEFANO CECCHI: And you Father Confessor Paolo Ricordati are a born politician.

ANTONIO: Then we're going to stay? Mother Jesus be praised. Excuse me, gracious sires, but I must... (*He heads in the direction of the NUNS*) Oh, Ladies! Ladies!

PROVOST STEFANO CECCHI: Antonio! (*But it's too late to stop him. Antonio has put his hands together in prayer position and is running toward the sound of the chanting nuns. The PROVOST and FATHER talk as they walk off.*) If you ever tire of shepherding these women about come round and see me. There'll be a post waiting for you in my government.

FATHER PAOLO RICORDATI: (*Crossing himself and reciting*) In nomine Patrie, Filii, et Spritus Sancti....

(*They exit*)

End of Scene

ACT I, SCENE 2

(*THE NEXT DAY. The Reading Room. BENEDETTA and BARTOLOMEA talk. BENEDETTA does not wear her abbess robe.*)

BENEDETTA: Everything's gotten so complicated, hasn't it? It was different when it all began. Peaceful. Joyous. And my papa-- how he loved me. We would walk the mountains of the Arno River Valley hand in hand, while he taught me the Rosary and to pray in Latin. He told me stories of Saint Catherine of Siena. No girl ever had such a papa. (*Beat*) Oh, how I long to see him. It's been years. I was a very little girl when he took my hand in his and we walked the roads and valleys into Pescia. I understand why he doesn't come. He has the farm to watch over and such a journey would keep him away too long from my mother. But he must think of me. Once in awhile. Don't you think, Bartolomea?

BARTOLOMEA: (*Pause*) Benedetta. Maybe-- maybe you shouldn't continue.

BENEDETTA: What?

BARTOLOMEA: Well, Provost Cecchi, he.... You could--
(Cautious. She knows this isn't going to go over well.) take it back.

BENEDETTA: What are you saying to me?

BARTOLOMEA: No, wait. Listen a moment. I'm sure the Provost would forgive you if you only....

BENEDETTA: Forgive me for what? Have you and I gone this far and now you doubt me?

BARTOLOMEA: No. No, never. I would never doubt you, but if harm were to come to you I...

BENEDETTA: *(Looking out the window)* Look. The children of Pescia. They play here everyday now. Right outside the convent walls. I love watching them. Their parents send them. Do you know why they do this?

BARTOLOMEA: Yes. To be close to you, to receive blessings from you. And protection. Where you are no plague can be for God would not allow it. I know. But this is all getting too dangerous. When they ask me their questions I get so frightened I'll say the wrong thing and...

BENEDETTA: What wrong thing?

BARTOLOMEA: *(Beat)* You know.

BENEDETTA: No. I don't. *(Beat)* Bartolomea, I was born for this. On the night of my birth it was arranged. My dear Mother had not been able to bring any living children into the world before me. And on that night when she was to be delivered, the mid wife hurried to papa who waited with wringing hands in the adjoining room. She told him to prepare himself, another child's death was at hand. Papa threw himself to his knees in front of the fire that burned in our fireplace and cried out, "Oh, Lord, save this child and I will dedicate its life to You and You alone." As the sun completed its revolution around the earth and was full over our mountains God's hand reached down from His home in the heavens and yanked me into this life. As he did not fail me then, He will not fail me now. Little one, keep faith.

End of Scene

ACT I, SCENE 3

(Sound of women singing Gregorian Chants. FIORA, BAR-TOLOMEA, BENEDETTA and CATERINA enter their heads bowed. They fall to their knees, their hands in prayer position. FATHER PAOLO enters. He makes the sign of the cross over the wine chalice that he holds; he takes a sip. He makes the sign of the cross over the host. He places a host on each nun's tongue and makes the sign of the cross over each head. Each nun after receiving the host bows her head in prayer. FATHER PAOLO and the PROVOST go to the side to consult with each other. ANTONIO creeps over to CATERINA.)

ANTONIO: Psst. Caterina.

CATERINA: *(CATERINA keeps her hands in prayer position, speaks softly)* Away arrant knave with your perverse inclinations. I am at prayer.

ANTONIO: *(ANTONIO runs his hand over her rear)*. Do you not want my perverse inclination to lie within your hinder parts?

CATERINA: *(Without removing ANTONIO's hand, CATERINA keeps her hands in prayer position, shaking.)* Desist, foul devil. Oh, God, preserve my soul. *(CATERINA's breath quickens, but trying to hang on as ANTONIO continues to touch her).* Oh, Lord, I do truly, truly love---love thee, but, but...

ANTONIO: Oh, chaste treasure, let my carrot pick your lock.

CATERINA: Meet me in the refectory closet in a few minutes. God forgive me. *(She genuflects to crucifix and hurries off.)*

ANTONIO: Bless you, fair maiden! *(He runs in the opposite direction)*

PROVOST STEFANO CECCHI: Where are you rushing off to? I still have need of you.

ANTONIO: Oh. Well, uh.... *(ANTONIO grabs himself)* Piss! I must sire! It pains me so!

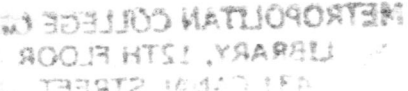

36

PROVOST STEFANO CECCHI: Surely, the world will come to an end, the earth uprooted from its place in the center of the universe and the heavens turned upside down all because of piss. Well, if you must you must. Empty yourself and return posthaste.

ANTONIO: *(ANTONIO runs off, still holding himself)* Yes, sire!

PROVOST STEFANO CECCHI: And so Father, let us continue. Tell me.

FATHER PAOLO RICORDATI: Soon the day of Benedetta's wedding arrived. And there was much excitement and preparation.

(CATERINA sets a center chair and drapes it in a red blanket. She puts two empty chairs on either side of it.)

BARTOLOMEA: *(To FIORA as she hurries off with other nuns)* And did you hear? Even the Archangel Gabriel is coming. And with his trumpet.

FATHER PAOLO RICORDATI: The convent doors were thrown wide to receive the townspeople who had walked days upon days so that they might witness the wedding of their blessed Benedetta to our Lord.

(Mystical music plays. BENEDETTA, wearing her Abbess cloak, walks down the audience aisle with a beautiful long wedding veil on her head. She throws flowers at the crowds. FIORA carries her long train. She is headed toward the stage where FATHER PAOLO and PROVOST stand on the stage off to the side. ANTONIO returns to write in his book. BARTOLOMEA enters stage in a rush, calling to BENEDETTA. She wears large wings.)

BARTOLOMEA: Benedetta, wait, wait. Don't start without me. These wings are so big.

(She half flies, half wobbles toward BENEDETTA. BENEDETTA passes out flowers to people in the audience and ab libs talking to them. She says things like. "Thank you for coming. God will bless you this day. May the plague never find you. How is your family? Your children? I will send my prayers unto you . Have a flower from Jesus." With great dignity, BENEDETTA mounts the stage. SHE puts out HER hand, but suddenly she covers her eyes with her hands and falls to her knees.)

BENEDETTA: Oh, Lord! Such a blinding light you shed. I can barely look and yet I must. It pierces through my eyes straight into my mind.

(CATERINA, FIORA and BARTOLOMEA fall to their knees).

PROVOST STEFANO CECCHI: *(To FATHER)* You see anything?

BENEDETTA: *(Taking her hands away from her eyes)* I see. More deeply do I see than I have ever seen before. I see you wrapped in the light of a bursting star. I see you with your mother, the Blessed Virgin and with dear St. Catherine of Siena who guides me always. And with all the angels!

ANTONIO: Where? Where?

PROVOST STEFANO CECCHI: Shut up, you plague sore and keep writing.

BENEDETTA: That there could be so much love here is a miracle beyond measure. Have mercy Lord on these dear people who have given up a day's work to see us wed. *(She stands, facing the crowd. Her voice becomes deeper, less her own. When she moves, she moves more like a man.)* My dear ones, do not think that Benedetta speaks of herself. I speak through her. This day Benedetta, I shall marry you. *(In her usual voice)* Oh, but, Lord, I am not worthy that you should honor me so.*(In her deeper voice)* I have a ring that I want you to wear always. *(BENEDETTA takes out an invisible ring and holds it up.)*

FIORA: Oh, look, the ring! See how it sparkles in the light. Let me see, Benedetta. Let me see.

ANTONIO: I bet its real gold.

BENEDETTA: *(In her usual voice as she puts the ring on her finger)* But let it not be according to my will, but thy will be done.

PROVOST STEFANO CECCHI: Oh, well, this is ridiculous. There's no one there. *(Beat)* Is there?

FATHER PAOLO RICORDATI: And did I not teach you the words of Jesus who said to Thomas, "Blessed is he who does not see and yet believes."

PROVOST STEFANO CECCHI: Then, you think maybe she....? How can she be? She's from the mountains.

FATHER PAOLO RICORDATI: And is it not written, "Can any good come out of Nazareth?"

PROVOST STEFANO CECCHI: Then you really do believe her?

ANTONIO: *I* believe her.

PROVOST STEFANO CECCHI: Well, of course, *you* do. Keep writing.

FATHER PAOLO RICORDATI: Shsh. She's going to speak.

BENEDETTA: *(Sitting now in the center chair, speaking in the deeper voice)* Now, as my wife, I instruct Benedetta to be patient and pure in all things. She must set a good example for the town and the sisters. Most importantly, she must obey her superiors who will guide her in all things righteous. Oh, dear, sinners, you must follow my bride for she has been given great gifts by me who loves her. She can intervene for you. If you do not stir her wrath. But Sinners, woe unto you who do not believe. A great plague will befall this town if....

(The NUNS and ANTONIO gasp. They cross themselves hurriedly.)

PROVOST STEFANO CECCHI: What is this? No, I will not have it. A Mother Abbess threatening my town, myself. No! Go home! All of you.

FIORA: But good Provost what if she does bring plague? May God forbid. *(Crosses herself)* I have lost my whole family to the one that rages now in Palermo.

CATERINA: They've just moved my brother to the pest house.

PROVOST STEFANO CECCHI: Silence! There will be no plague here. I shall not allow it.

FATHER PAOLO RICORDATI: Won't you, Stefano?

PROVOST STEFANO CECCHI: *(Beat)* Go! All of you. To your chambers. You too, Antonio. Go home. And talk of this to no one.

ANTONIO: Yes, sire. *(ANTONIO runs over to CATERINA)* My lady, fair Caterina!

PROVOST STEFANO CECCHI: *(To ANTONIO)* No one.

ANTONIO: Yes, sire.

(Everyone starts to exit in silence. The lights move into the present. All signs of the wedding are quickly whisked away by the exiting nuns. There is no sign of BENEDETTA's wedding veil as she exits.)

PROVOST STEFANO CECCHI: *(To BENEDETTA)* Wait! You! (*The PROVOST stares at her a moment as if trying to see inside of her.*)

BENEDETTA: Sire?

PROVOST: Who *are* you?

BENEDETTA: *(Gently) That*, dear, Provost, is it what we are here to find out. Is it not?

PROVOST STEFANO CECCHI: *(Pause)* Go! Go! Get out of here!

BENEDETTA: As you will, Sire. *(She bows slightly and exits calmly with great dignity).*

FATHER PAOLO RICORDATI: Stefano, will you chase me home, too?

PROVOST STEFANO CECCHI: What was I to do? She's been rousing the town, the convent. I had to put a stop to it.

FATHER PAOLO RICORDATI: Have a glass of port. *(FATHER hands him a glass of port.)*

PROVOST STEFANO CECCHI: That woman! She will make me take leave my senses!

FATHER PAOLO RICORDATI: Yes, she has been known to have that effect. Stefano, haven't you completed your investigation yet? Do you still think she is such a terrible threat to you? She's a girl. But she is well loved in the town. They don't like that you've removed her from her position and keep her locked up behind cloister walls.

PROVOST STEFANO CECCHI: *(Pause)* Have you read The Sun Spot Letters by the mathematician, Galileo Galilei?

FATHER PAOLO RICORDATI: Sorry, no. I've never heard of the man.

PROVOST STEFANO CECCHI: Well, in this book, he explains the Copernican proposition that the sun does not revolve around the earth; but rather the earth revolves around the sun.

FATHER PAOLO RICORDATI: That's ridiculous. It clearly states in the Bible, "The sun also riseth and the sun goeth down and hastens to its place where it arose."

PROVOST STEFANO CECCHI: I know, but listen. He also says that our dear home, our earth, is not firmly planted in the center of the firmament. But is rolling about at enormous speeds, rolling about with other celestial bodies. Of course, he clearly states this is merely a hypothesis, but...

FATHER PAOLO RICORDATI: What it sounds like is blasphemy and heresy. You best stop reading the words of this man, this, uh, uh....

PROVOST STEFANO CECCHI: Galileo.

FATHER PAOLO RICORDATI: You best be done with him if you truly value your soul. If the Office of the Inquisition were to hear...

PROVOST STEFANO CECCHI: Will you listen to me one moment! One moment without bias. My head pains me with thinking and there's no one to say it to!

FATHER PAOLO RICORDATI: What is it, Stefano? What troubles you so?

PROVOST STEFANO CECCHI: *(Pause)* What if this man's hypothesis *is* correct?

FATHER PAOLO RICORDATI: But it's not correct. Think, Stefano, for your soul's sake, think! If we were moving around and around through the sky how is it we can remain standing in one place without falling over. You complicate things. You always did.

PROVOST STEFANO CECCHI: Paolo, sometimes-- sometimes I fear it *is* true. That the earth is not planted firmly in the center of the universe, but rolls about the sun in some insane chaotic flight. And if that is true there is no firm place where *I* can plant my feet. No place, Paolo. Nowhere.

FATHER PAOLO RICORDATI: *(Beat)* I-- don't understand. I don't know how to help you.

PROVOST STEFANO CECCHI: *(Pause)* *You* believe her, don't you? *(Beat)* You do. I see it in your eyes. I hear it in your voice whenever you talk of her. And who knows maybe you're right. Maybe she is. *(Pause)* Wouldn't that be wonderful, Paolo? Wouldn't that be absolutely wonderful?

End of Act I

ACT II, SCENE 1

(In the black out there is the sound of a door chime. BENEDETTA goes to answer the door. She wears her Abbess cloak. FATHER RICORDATI waits at the doorway. The PROVOST and ANTONIO stand to the side. ANTONIO takes notes.)

BENEDETTA: You've come, of course, about the new appointment to the Board of Directors for the convent. I think Lorenzo Pagni would be a good choice. He's a man of wealth who has always looked favorably upon this convent.

FATHER PAOLO RICORDATI: Yes, Benedetta, you are right. As always. Pagni is a good man and I will inform the Board of your advice this very evening, but-- this is not the reason I came to see you today. I don't know how to... Even as a cleric one is never certain how to proceed in these matters. There's been news. I...

BENEDETTA: Father, you look distressed. Take heart. Jesus brings comfort.

FATHER PAOLO RICORDATI: Yes. Benedetta, there's been a letter from Velano. Your father-- he has died. (*BENEDETTA stumbles back, almost losing her balance.*)

BARTOLOMEA: Benedetta, are you all right?

BENEDETTA: Fine, fine.

FATHER PAOLO RICORDATI: *(To BARTOLOMEA)* Bring water. Quick girl.

(BARTOLOMEA starts to run.)

BENEDETTA: No.

(BARTOLOMEA stops short.)

BENEDETTA: I am fine. Christ, my husband, knows what is best. Bartolomea, prepare the other sisters for my sermon. I will preach today.

BARTOLOMEA: But...

BENEDETTA: Please do as I say. Thank you, Good Father for your news. Now, if you'll excuse me...

FATHER PAOLO RICORDATI: If there is anything I can do to help you...

BENEDETTA: Good day.

(FATHER RICORDATI makes the sign of the cross over BENEDETTA and exits. Benedetta wobbles as she walks.)

PROVOST STEFANO CECCHI: *(To BARTOLOMEA)* Did she preach that day?

BARTOLOMEA: Well...

(BENEDETTA looks as if she is having trouble breathing. She runs into her cell, throws off her cloak, grabs a salami that is hidden behind a chair. She gulps down large chunks of it. FIORA and CATERINA peek around the corner at her.)

FIORA: Look! Look, Caterina, didn't I tell you? See! She eats a whole salami. She hides it in her cell and when she thinks no one is looking she gorges herself. Fasting, hah!

CATERINA: When will you leave her alone, Fiora? *(CATERINA moves toward BENEDETTA)* Benedetta? May I be of some service to you?

(BENEDETTA looks up at her like a scared rabbit; she runs off stage. We hear the sound of vomiting.)

FIORA: *(To CATERINA)* See? See? *(To PROVOST)* See, Provost? I saw her with my very own two eyes stuffing herself and then throwing it up again. Now, tell me this. What kind of fasting is that?

CATERINA: Will you stop. She had just lost her beloved father that day. Have some pity, Fiora. Provost, surely, there is a place for some human pity in all this. Is there not?

FIORA: I thought she was supposed to be some sort of great mystic.

CATERINA: And a mystic may not mourn. Where is that written? Provost?

FIORA: And is she the only one to lose her family? Even you have lost your brother in Palermo and yet you do not...

CATERINA: Will you never tire of this jealous tirade against Benedetta? Remember, she has the power to get you extra time in purgatory.

FIORA: What do you think about that?

PROVOST STEFANO CECCHI: Yes, Caterina. What do *you* think about that?

CATERINA: I don't.

PROVOST STEFANO CECCHI: Surely, you must have thoughts about her powers.

CATERINA: I don't. Benedetta never gives me any troubles.

FIORA: Well, she gives *me* plenty. I get tired of hearing how I am a sinner and *she* is some sort of Saint. I'm not voting her in as abbess at the next election.

CATERINA: Do you know what you're saying? It's because of Benedetta the town gives us respect and its wealthy patrons buy our silk. We eat more regularly than we ever did before Benedetta. Show some gratitude. *(BENEDETTA enters. She walks with strength and dignity.)*

BENEDETTA: (BENEDETTA *nods at the women*) Sisters? (*She kneels to pray*) Oh, God, God, I am not worthy! Not fit to be your bride. Passions and desires assault me daily. I fear I will infect your dear children with the plague boils that inhabit my mind?

FIORA: *(To CATERINA)* See? She condemns herself.

CATERINA: Why do you-- all of you-- keep expecting her to be normal? She's a mystic for mercy sake. She's *supposed* to be odd. May God forgive us! *(She crosses herself and exits in disgust.)*

BENEDETTA: *(She grabs her flagellation stick and hits herself hard).* Lord, courage, give me courage, that I might deserve you. *(She wacks herself again. It is obvious that this is painful. She does it again and again.)*

(BARTOLOMEA enters.)

BARTOLOMEA: Benedetta, no, stop. It is not the hour of discipline. Don't do it more.

BENEDETTA: No! Not too close. My mind burns. I am filled with dirt, dear one. I must wash it from me. *(She dunks a cloth in a bowl of water and scrubs herself with it)* Splenditello haunts me daily now, Bartolomea.

PROVOST STEFANO CECCHI: *(To BARTOLOMEA)* Who?!

BARTOLOMEA: Oh. Splenditello. He's Benedetta's guardian angel that Jesus charged with her instruction. He's a beautiful young man who carries a staff. On one side there are flowers and on the other side thorns. When Benedetta's thoughts are pure Splenditello touches her ever so lightly with his flowers. But when her thoughts are impure he beats her ferociously with his thorns.

PROVOST STEFANO CECCHI: *(To FATHER PAOLO)* You knew about this Splen, splen...?

BARTOLOMEA: Ditello.

PROVOST STEFANO CECCHI: Yes. You knew?

FATHER PAOLO RICORDATI: Well--Benedetta had mentioned something about him to me, yes.

PROVOST STEFANO CECCHI: Had she? And you never told me?

FATHER PAOLO RICORDATI: It never seemed very important.

PROVOST STEFANO CECCHI: Not important? We're here to prove whether this woman is a true mystic, something from the devil or an out and out fraud and she calls some spirit Splendi, splendi.

BARTOLOMEA: Ditello.

PROVOST STEFANO CECCHI: Didn't that sound the least bit demonic to you?

FATHER PAOLO RICORDATI: Benedetta is not from the devil.

BARTOLOMEA: No. She is holy, blessed by God.

BENEDETTA: Bartolomea, he beats me mercilessly now. I can hardly stand it. I must wash and wash and wash.

BARTOLOMEA: *(To BENEDETTA)* But you impure? That is not possible. *(To PROVOST)* It isn't *(To BENEDETTA)* Oh, but the Father Confessor. He's waiting for you. He cannot begin to hear the confessions without you. Benedetta, please. You can't keep him waiting.

BENEDETTA: All right! (*BENEDETTA puts on her cloak and walks with firmness to FATHER PAOLO*) Father Paolo. How good of you to come.

FATHER PAOLO RICORDATI: My dear Benedetta. I did not expect to be kept waiting.

PROVOST STEFANO CECCHI: Well, at least, you properly chastised her.

FATHER PAOLO RICORDATI: Of course.

BENEDETTA: And neither should you be kept waiting. I humbly beg your pardon.

FATHER PAOLO RICORDATI: And, of course, you have it. I cannot deny you anything, which may lead to both our destructions.

PROVOST STEFANO CECCHI: Yes.

(The two men eye each other).

BARTOLOMEA: Father Paolo heard the confessions of the sisters. And as was his custom he left so that the sisters may complete their daily flagellation.

(FIORA runs in.)

FIORA: She had no right. I saw her Monsignor Provost. She made us whip ourselves to the bone, but she barely touched herself.

BARTOLOMEA: Not true. Not true, Monsignor Provost. How can you make up such stories?

FATHER PAOLO RICORDATI: It is a sin to judge others during mortification of the flesh.

BARTOLOMEA: Benedetta beats herself the hardest. She does it when she doesn't even have to, when she's alone in her cell.

FIORA: I'm no liar! I know what I saw. You can bet Benedetta sent this one to tell you these lies.

BARTOLOMEA: She did not!

PROVOST STEFANO CECCHI: Stop, stop! Why didn't you tell anyone what you saw?

FIORA: I did. I told *him*. *(She points at FATHER RICORDATI)*

PROVOST STEFANO CECCHI: Is this true, Paolo?

FATHER PAOLO RICORDATI: Well, I'm not sure I can recall, uh... these events were awhile ago and...

FIORA: Surely, you remember I came to you. You said I should speak my mind in front of the others in the refectory. You were there when I did.

FATHER PAOLO RICORDATI: But I don't seem... I'm not quite sure I.... It's all somewhat vague and...

FIORA: Not to me it isn't.

(The NUNS and FATHER PAOLO gather around the table. They say a silent grace, cross themselves. They eat a moment in silence. FIORA stands.)

FIORA: Mother Abbess.

BENEDETTA: So formal, *Sister* Fiora.

FIORA: Today during flagellation you directed us to beat ourselves harder than usual.

BENEDETTA: As Jesus directed.

FIORA: And yet-- you barely touched yourself.

BENEDETTA: It is a sin to judge others during flagellation. Sit down.

FIORA: I shall not.

BENEDETTA: You question my leadership?

FIORA: I do.

BENEDETTA: I see. Then, something must be done. Should I step down as your Abbess?

FIORA: I didn't say that. I just meant...

BENEDETTA: Poll the others. See if they think I should step down.

FIORA: I didn't say that. I only meant to point out...

BENEDETTA: *(She takes out whipping switch.)* What did you mean to point out?

FIORA: Uh, uh...

BENEDETTA: The devil has taken up residence in your soul, Sister. He wants to create disorder in our house and I shall not have it. He must be cast out. Now. Take this stick and cast him out of yourself.

FIORA: What?

BENEDETTA: *(Holding stick out toward FIORA)* Flagellate yourself with this stick.

FIORA: Now? By myself? In front of the others? Even Father?

BENEDETTA: As the Lord wills.

FIORA: But... Sisters?

(They avert their eyes.)

BENEDETTA: Do not look to your sisters to help you. Obedience to God and earthly authority must be kept or we are doomed. Your Sisters know that. Take the stick. Scourge the whole of your body until your spirit is brought back into abeyance with God's will.

FIORA: Father, will you not speak for me? It is because of you that I... *(Father RICORDATI averts his eyes.)* Caterina?

CATERINA: *(With head bowed)* Obedience is our holiest vow, Sister Fiora. It keeps our world from dissolving into chaos.

BENEDETTA: The stick, Sister Fiora.

(FIORA slowly reaches toward the stick and takes it from BENEDETTA).

BARTOLOMEA *(Rising)* I have to go.

BENEDETTA: Stay where you are. Fiora, proceed.

(FIORA hits herself lightly on the arm)

BENEDETTA: Harder. Show Jesus you mean it.

(FIORA hits herself harder on the arm)

BENEDETTA: Harder! Harder!

(FIORA hits herself hard so that the sound of the whip can be heard. Her face shows pain.)

BENEDETTA: Better. Now, your back. Scourge your back. Scourge it as Christ's back was scourged.

FIORA: *(Softly)* Benedetta, please. Not in front of the others. Have pity. They're all looking at me.

BENEDETTA: As they should. Mortification always takes place in front of others. It makes us humble. Continue. *(FIORA hits herself hard and angrily on the back. It is as if she were hitting BENEDETTA.)* Good. More! More! Harder! Harder! *(Spurred on by BENEDETTA, FIORA beats herself harder and harder.)* Yes! Harder! Harder! More! More! Harder! Harder!*(The others around the table flinch with the sound.)* Down. On the floor. Kiss the floor in repentance. *(FIORA gets onto all fours and kisses the floor. BENEDETTA takes the stick from FIORA's hands and is about to beat her in the rear with it. BARTOLOMEA jumps up. BENEDETTA freezes mid swing.)*

BARTOLOMEA: No! Monsignor Provost. No! That never happened. Benedetta would *never* hit...

PROVOST STEFANO CECCHI: Quiet! You had your turn! Continue!

BENEDETTA: *(She completes her swing and hits FIORA)* Walk, dog! Walk like a dog, you roast meat for worms. *(FIORA follows the instructions as BENEDETTA continues to hit her on the rear with the stick).* Bark, bark like a dog. *(FIORA barks softly)* Louder. Bark so the Heavens hear. Bark! Bark! *(BENEDETTA beats FIORA in the rear as FIORA makes loud barking sounds.)*

BARTOLOMEA: *(More desperate)* No, Monsignor, please, you must not believe this. This did not happen. Fiora struck herself, yes. As she should, in repentance for her disobedience, but Benedetta *never* struck her. No. Rather, she reached out her hand to Fiora and...

(FIORA takes the stick and hits herself hard).

BENEDETTA: *(BENEDETTA reaches out to FIORA)* Fiora, give me the stick. It is enough now. It is enough. Go. Rest yourself. *(Fearfully FIORA gives the stick to BENEDETTA.)*

(There is a moment of warmth between BENEDETTA and FIORA. Then FIORA jumps out of it).

FIORA: Rest myself? Rest myself?! When did Benedetta ever say such a thing to me?

PROVOST STEFANO CECCHI: Caterina?

CATERINA: Benedetta showed Fiora a great many kindnesses.

FIORA: When? When? When did she ever love me like you?

CATERINA: You are too filled with jealousy.

FIORA: Oh, I see how this is to be. You will all conspire against me, but Mother Jesus knows I speak the truth.

BENEDETTA: *(Coming up behind FIORA and hitting her hard in the rear)* Yes, bark, bark! *(FIORA falls to all fours)* Wag your tail. Wag your tail, foul plague dog! Walk! Bark! Walk! Wag your tail! *(FIORA, crying, and barking walks like a dog wagging her tail, while BENEDETTA beats her in the rear.)*

PROVOST STEFANO CECCHI: Paolo?

FATHER PAOLO RICORDATI: Stefano, you have to understand. The situation with Benedetta. It was all very difficult. Her visions and moods so changeable that I, I... Once I came upon her alone. She didn't know I watched.

(The lights focus on BENEDETTA so that she glows with a heavenly beauty. She stares in a beatific ecstasy. Father Paolo stands in shadow, totally captivated.)

BENEDETTA: *(BENEDETTA speaks to a vision)* My Lord.

FATHER PAOLO RICORDATI: And when I saw her face I was certain. Certain she saw what could not be seen with mere eyes. I am a simple country preacher, but this-- this... How could Holy Mother Church expect me to, to...I tried. I tried, Stefano.

PROVOST STEFANO CECCHI: *(The PROVOST takes a few steps toward Benedetta, but stops before moving into her light. He speaks to Father, but looks at Benedetta.)* You saw her Paolo? Alone with our Lord?

FATHER PAOLO RICORDATI: Yes.

PROVOST STEFANO CECCHI: Yes. *(Pause)* Then, perhaps, the earth remains at the center, planted and firm. Do you think, Paolo?

FATHER PAOLO RICORDATI: Yes. I do.

FIORA: (*Approaching BENEDETTA's circle of light, but not in it.*) Why *you*? Why would Christ choose *you*? Why am *I* never the one who is chosen?

BENEDETTA: Come, Fiora. Come. You have been hurt.

(*BENEDETTA holds out her arms for FIORA; FIORA mesmerized moves toward BENEDETTA, wanting to accept the warmth*).

FIORA: (*FIORA breaks the spell.*) No. I have no mother, no father. (*To Provost*) And that's not all, Provost. (*The light on BENEDETTA blinks off. The Provost comes back from his reverie to listen to FIORA.*) I saw the two of *them*. We were all talking before it was time to chant Lauds.

(*BARTOLOMEA, CATERINA and BENEDETTA enter giggling among themselves. BENEDETTA collapses. The woman gather around her, shocked and frightened*).

BARTOLOMEA: Benedetta, what is it? Should I go for the Father Confessor?

(*CATERINA kneels close to BENEDETTA, holding her wrist, feeling her pulse.*

PROVOST STEFANO CECCHI: But you'd seen this sort of thing many times. Why so alarmed?

FIORA: It came upon her suddenly with no warning. It had never come like this before. It appeared that, that she might be... (*To CATERINA*) Caterina, you don't think she's...? (*CATERINA drops BENEDETTA's arm and crosses herself. FIORA crosses herself.*) Oh, Mother in Heaven. I hope I didn't offend her. Do you think I offended her? Go for the Father. He'll know what to do.

BARTOLOMEA: (Running off) Father! Father Confessor! Come quick! Come quick!!(*BARTOLOMEA runs off. In a few moments FATHER PAOLO runs on, BARTOLOMEA following behind.*) See! You've got to save her.

FIORA: Father, Jesus has come and taken our dear Benedetta away from us.

FATHER PAOLO RICORDATI: Go! To your cells! All of you, go!

(They start to scurry off.)

BARTOLOMEA: Please. Father, save her.

CATERINA: Come, dear. *(CATERINA guides BARTOLOMEA off).*

FATHER PAOLO RICORDATI: *(FATHER RICORDATI speaks more forcefully than we have ever seen him.)* Benedetta! Come back to life! Now!

BENEDETTA: *(BENEDETTA rises)* Father, why so frightened? Hold fast to your faith. Surely, you know I must walk in the garden of our Lord.

FATHER PAOLO RICORDATI: *(FATHER RICORDATI grabs her.)* Stop it! You must stop it. They are coming for you! Benedetta, do you not know what they can do to you?

BENEDETTA: Nothing that Jesus does not allow, good Father. Where has your faith gone off to?

FATHER PAOLO RICORDATI: Stop it! Stop it, I tell you! Don't you know? Don't you know?

(FATHER RICORDATI kisses BENEDETTA passionately. BENEDETTA allows herself to be kissed, but does not respond. FATHER stops kissing her, backs away, not looking at her.)

FIORA: *(To PROVOST)* And that's just what happened, Sire.

PROVOST STEFANO CECCHI: Paolo?

FATHER PAOLO RICORDATI: No. She did not see correctly. She was looking from over there. It may have appeared that I--I... *(Having difficulty getting the word out)* kissed. But no. I could not. I was very concerned about Benedetta's health, yes, and so I stood close and it may have seemed from there, but... Stop, looking at me like that! It was like this. Go over there. Look from there. You'll see.

(The PROVOST goes to the place. FATHER PAOLO goes to BENEDETTA). Like this. I stood thus. To check her health. Close, but I never touched. But from there it may have looked... I think--think it was like this. My memory is not what it once was. But I'm sure... I never would have done that! I couldn't have. She's a girl, I am an old man! I never, ever... I took holy vows. Everyone is expecting too much of me. How could Jesus give me this impossible task? How can anyone do this? She is like my own child. That's what my love is for her, not this other. You cannot accuse me. She is holy. A holy woman sent by God. I am her protector. Jesus chose me to, to...You cannot--CANNOT accuse me of, of...*(HE shakes with holding back tears that are starting to break through. Everyone stares at him.)*

BENEDETTA: My poor good Father Paolo, don't worry. Jesus has already forgiven you.

End of scene

ACT II, SCENE 2

(Late at night. The room is in shadow except for the candle that burns on the desk where the PROVOST pours over the days' notes. BENEDETTA enters quietly. She wears a robe.)

BENEDETTA: I see we have much in common. The shadows of night keep me awake too.

PROVOST STEFANO CECCHI: Mother. I was just finishing up some work, but it is time now that I was off to my home. *(The PROVOST gathers up his papers and starts to go.)*

BENEDETTA: Have you seen the moon tonight?

PROVOST STEFANO CECCHI: Well, no, I haven't. I often get too busy with affairs of state to remember the moon. At least, in the way you mean it.

BENEDETTA: Come. Look, now. Through this window. See how she sits rounder and bigger, I think, than I have ever seen her. Quiet and unconcerned right on top of that hill. The town sleeps so it may be that we are the only two people to see her tonight.

PROVOST STEFANO CECCHI: Looking at the moon like this makes none of it matter so very much. Whether the sun revolves around us or we around it. Whether we are floating or stuck. *(Beat)* I feel peaceful standing here beside you. I never feel peaceful.

BENEDETTA: And I must repair to my bedchamber, though I rarely sleep. The walls may have eyes to see with and tongues to speak with. And we could become their very next topic. Good night, Monsignor Provost. Safe journey to your home.

PROVOST: Good night, Mother. *(She starts to exit)* Mother? *(She stops).* I—I want to say—to tell you that—I—hope...that I—want.... Sleep well.

(SHE smiles, nods and exits.)

End of scene

ACT II, SCENE 3

(The next day. The NUNS sing their morning devotions off stage. THE PROVOST and ANTONIO go over the records of the investigation. FATHER PAOLO enters, but does not look at the PROVOST.)

PROVOST STEFANO CECCHI: Good morning, Paolo. I trust you slept well.

FATHER PAOLO RICORDATI: No. To be frank I did not.

PROVOST STEFANO CECCHI: *(To Antonio)* Find the place. *(The PROVOST goes to FATHER PAOLO.)* You came early. You must have risen before the sun as Antonio and I did. We may have some good news for you shortly. *(He is disturbed by FATHER PAOLO's unjovial silence)* You know, Paolo, no one cares whom you desire or whom you fornicate with for that matter. I, myself, just between you and me-- I wouldn't want this getting out-- but I have had a nun now and again. It is to be expected. It is as nothing.

FATHER PAOLO RICORDATI: But I never... I know many of the religious have done those sorts of things. There was that incident a few years ago that they sent you to investigate with the monks and nuns of Santa Chiara. But me? No, Stefano.

PROVOST STEFANO CECCHI: And you still haven't, no? Well, what's one little kiss, heh?

FATHER PAOLO RICORDATI: I never kissed her. I wouldn't do that. You must believe me. When I was a boy in Florence I knew even then I would give my life to God. I have never strayed from my vows. Not in deed or in --thought. And then—Benedetta...

ANTONIO: I found it, sire.

PROVOST STEFANO CECCHI: Let me see.

FATHER PAOLO RICORDATI: What?

PROVOST STEFANO CECCHI: The testimony on that angel-- Splenditello.

FATHER PAOLO RICORDATI: Is there some problem?

PROVOST STEFANO CECCHI: Everything else seems in order. I'm only a little troubled by this Splenditello fellow. He doesn't quite fit with what one would expect. Nothing like him is in the writings of St. Catherine of Siena or St. Teresa of Avila. Still, it's probably nothing. A little fleck in a perfect picture.

FATHER PAOLO RICORDATI: What do you mean?

PROVOST STEFANO CECCHI: Whether you kissed Benedetta or not doesn't much matter. What does matter is that Sister Fiora made it quite clear that Benedetta did not kiss you. This refusal of sensuality, along with the witnesses to her visions and the stigmata all work in her favor. Recall last year's papal bull, which canonized Saint Teresa of Avila. One of the main points made in that document was that Saint Teresa had overcome her woman's nature through the refusal of sensuality and by so doing had become a man. I think the same might be applied to Benedetta.

FATHER PAOLO RICORDATI: Are you saying what I can only hope to hear?

PROVOST STEFANO CECCHI: It appears that your Benedetta Carlini is the real thing. If all goes well with the last of my questioning today I am prepared to complete my report this afternoon and recommend to the nuncio that Benedetta be allowed to continue as abbess of this convent and spiritual guide to Pescia.

FATHER PAOLO RICORDATI: Oh, Stefano I am so delighted. And relieved. I thought sure she was lost.

PROVOST STEFANO CECCHI: Why did you think that? Is there something I should know?

FATHER PAOLO RICORDATI: No! No, nothing. I'm just so happy my tongue got tied up in my teeth. Who will you question today?

PROVOST STEFANO CECCHI: Come forth Bartolomea Crivelli.

BARTOLOMEA: *(BARTOLOMEA enters with great hesitation)* But, good Monsignor, you've already questioned me. What can I tell you more?

PROVOST STEFANO CECCHI: Don't be frightened, girl. You know everyone here, Father Paolo, Antonio, myself, so there's no need to be timid. Sit. Just a few questions more and then you can go back to your reeling. Do you know what I want to speak to you about today?

BARTOLOMEA: Yes, sire. You told me yesterday at the seventeenth hour when the sun burned hot that you wanted to talk more about Splenditello. But I have nothing more to say about him so I don't see why...

PROVOST STEFANO CECCHI: What does he look like?

BARTOLOMEA: Look like, sire? Well, he—he occupies Benedetta's body.

PROVOST STEFANO CECCHI: Does he?

BARTOLOMEA: Sometimes.

PROVOST STEFANO CECCHI: Then he looks like Benedetta?

BARTOLOMEA: No. I mean, yes, no!

PROVOST STEFANO CECCHI: What does that mean? Are you trying to deceive us?

BARTOLOMEA: No, sire! I would never do that! It's just that it's difficult—difficult to explain.

PROVOST STEFANO CECCHI: You best begin explaining. You do know the penalty for lying to this investigation, don't you? Imprisonment for life.

BARTOLOMEA: No! I did nothing.

FATHER PAOLO RICORDATI: Stefano, don't threaten this girl.

PROVOST STEFANO CECCHI: It is no threat. We must discover the truth. Speak, Sister.

FATHER PAOLO RICORDATI: You have your truth already. Your world is safe at its center. There is no need to go further.

PROVOST STEFANO CECCHI: The truth cannot be afraid or else it is not the truth. Speak, Sister.

BARTOLOMEA: I did nothing! Nothing, Monsignor.

PROVOST STEFANO CECCHI: Nothing? Nothing at all? Think, Sister. God knows your heart and will guide me to the truth.

BARTOLOMEA: I did nothing wrong! Nothing! He made me!

PROVOST STEFANO CECCHI: Who made you?

BARTOLOMEA: Oh, please, please, don't make me. I did nothing wrong. Benedetta, she... No! It was Splenditello. Jesus sent him to watch Benedetta and he promised someday—someday I'd be able to see him too just like Benedetta if only I--I...

PROVOST STEFANO CECCHI: Yes? Yes?

BARTOLOMEA: No! I don't remember.

PROVOST STEFANO CECCHI: What don't you remember? Speak, girl!

FATHER PAOLO RICORDATI: Stefano, I fear this will shake both our worlds. Stop now before it is too late.

BARTOLOMEA: Oh, please, please sire.

PROVOST STEFANO CECCHI: Speak, I tell you unless you require the help of the lash!

BARTOLOMEA: No!! The office. The sisters were singing. We shouldn't have been there then. Not during the prayers. (*Lights come up on BENEDETTA's office. BENEDETTA and BARTOLOMEA sneak in. BENDETTA wears her cloak.*) Oh, Benedetta, we shouldn't be here now. It's prayer time.

BENEDETTA: Shsh. This is fun. Exciting. No one knowing where we are. Time for your reading lesson!

BARTOLOMEA: Not now. If they catch us...

BENEDETTA: Don't worry. Open your book. Begin here. With Catherine of Siena's birth. (*She walks to the window to look out.*) Saint Catherine of Siena. She was so filled with heavenly wisdom that she was even an advisor to the church fathers. Imagine that. A woman advising the Holy Father. (*Beat*) I have a few things *I'd* like to say to him.

BARTOLOMEA Oh, no, Benedetta, please. We have enough troubles already.

BENEDETTA: My favorite story of Catherine is the one about the young convict boy, Niccolo. Catherine stayed by his side up to his very last breath of life. And when his head was separated from his body by the blade and was about to drop into the basket she caught it before it could fall. She clasped it to her breast and kissed it with her very own two lips as his blood dripped from her holy mouth.

BARTOLOMEA: What a beautiful story.

BENEDETTA: Yes. When I was small I, too dreamed of being a soldier for Christ. I dreamed I would ride one of Papa's horses into battle, my sword at my side. And I would draw my sword against the infidel. (*Acting out the scene*) And he would bow down and worship our Lord God. Such a child. The first time our Lord came to me was in my father's valley. As I sang on the banks of the Arno River he came to me in the guise of a nightingale. Together we sang and our music filled the whole valley. And my heart vibrated with him and I wanted for nothing. No longing was left in me except to love him more. He told me, that very day, all that was to transpire in my life. *(Pause)* Even the end. And he told me I must never be afraid and always keep faith. And so must you, Bartolomea. No matter what happens you must keep faith.

BARTOLOMEA: There was a time, Benedetta, when I used to think of this place as my prison. And then-- you.

BENEDETTA: Tell me, little bird. What did *you* dream of as a child? Marriage to some puffed up old man with piles of money?

BARTOLOMEA: No. I had no dreams for the future. I always knew this was where I would spend my days. My father was kind. He even paid a dowry so I could come here instead of ending up, well, you know, like those bad women. But I knew there would never be a marriage for me.

BENEDETTA: *(Cautiously)* You mean your mother and father weren't—married?

BARTOLOMEA: Does that bother you?

BENEDETTA: No. Of course not. My dear sweat Bartolomea. You are innocence itself. That you should have suffered these things makes my heart weep. *(She caresses BARTOLOMEA's head. They look deeply into each other's eyes. BENEDETTA kisses BARTOLOMEA on the mouth. BARTOLOMEA responds. ANTONIO drops his writing tablet with a loud thud.)*

ANTONIO: My notebook. *(ANTONIO picks it up. The men, in shock, move in and stand around the women.)*

BARTOLOMEA: No, no, that isn't what happened! Provost, Father, it wasn't like that. It was Splenditello. He was to blame. You must believe me. Not Benedetta. Not me.

PROVOST STEFANO CECCHI: Explain. Or prepare yourself for hell, girl.

(Lights come up on BENEDETTA's chamber. BENEDETTA lies on the bed, under a blanket.)

BARTOLOMEA: Yes, well, well.... Sometimes, at night, when the others slept Benedetta would be troubled with her visions and Splenditello would beat her with his thorns. Oh, it was so terrible for her and she'd be in the most horrible pain and she'd call out to me. *(To BENEDETTA)* What is it Benedetta?

BENEDETTA: Come closer. I have need of you. *(BARTOLOMEA goes to her. Bendetta throws off the blanket. She is naked or scantily clad, except for the veil on her head.)* Splenditello, bids me kiss you.

(BENEDETTA kisses BARTOLOMEA on the mouth. ANTONIO drops his notebook again.)

ANTONIO: My notebook!

PROVOST STEFANO CECCHI: *(To ANTONIO)* Pick up your paper and write, you clod of wayward marl!

(The men stand around the bed, horrified.)

BARTOLOMEA: *(Giggling and getting under the blanket with BENEDETTA)* Oh, we can't do this. It's a sin.

BENEDETTA: *(In the deeper, more masculine voice of Splenditello)* Not when an angel commands it.

BARTOLOMEA: Oh.

(BENEDETTA kisses BARTOLOMEA again. Then she climbs on top of BARTOLOMEA. They touch each other under the blanket, both obviously enjoying it. The men pace around the bed, extremely upset and shocked.)

ANTONIO: Girls can't do that! How'd they do it?

FATHER PAOLO RICORDATI: No, this is not possible. Not possible. Benedetta would never...

BARTOLOMEA: *(From her position under BENEDETTA)* Not Benedetta. Splenditello. *(BENEDETTA kisses BARTOLOMEA and touches her. BARTOLOMEA moans with pleasure.)*

BARTOLOMEA: I hated it, but he was an angel. What was I to do? No, not there, Splenditello.. Here. *(Beat)* Oh, yes!

PROVOST STEFANO CECCHI: How often did this occur?

BARTOLOMEA: Not often. Only three times a week.

(*ANTONIO drops his writing pad again. The PROVOST picks it up.*)

PROVOST STEFANO CECCHI: Will you stop dropping this book!

FATHER PAOLO RICORDATI: This is impossible! Impossible!

PROVOST STEFANO CECCHI: Stop saying that. *(Struggles to get words out.)* What, uh, what...? What instruments did you use?

BARTOLOMEA: Instruments? We didn't.

FATHER PAOLO: *(Crossing himself)* Oh, thank God and Mother in Heaven.

PROVOST STEFANO CECCHI: What did you do?!

ANTONIO: Yeah?! What?

BARTOLOMEA: Splenditello would lie atop me and, and...

FATHER PAOLO RICORDATI: Stefano, please. We don't need to know this. It's going too far.

PROVOST STEFANO CECCHI: We must know exactly what abomination occurred for the report. Benedetta lay atop you and...?

BARTOLOMEA: Not Benedetta. *(BENEDETTA and BARTOLOMEA move under a blanket touching each other.)* It was Splen, Splen... (*Both are building toward orgasm.*) Oh, Splenditello, I feel so, so... Oh, oh, oh.

FATHER PAOLO RICORDATI: *(To the women who are closer to orgasm.)* Stop that. Stop that now!

PROVOST STEFANO CECCHI: Tell us what you did! (*The women move into a long and extended orgasm. The men uncomfortably wait for them to finish.*) Well?!

BARTOLOMEA: *(Afterglow)* We corrupted ourselves.

PROVOST STEFANO CECCHI: *(To ANTONIO)* Don't you dare drop that thing again.

FATHER PAOLO RICORDATI: Romans 1:26! "Vile Affections! For even their women did change the natural use into that which is against nature!"

PROVOST STEFANO CECCHI: *(To BARTOLOMEA)* Do you know what you are saying, girl? You're talking sodomy. That is punishable by death. By burning.

BARTOLOMEA: *(Jumping out of bed)* No! Not me! Splenditello. He made me.

PROVOST STEFANO CECCHI: Splenditello or Benedetta made you?

BARTOLOMEA: Splenditello.

(The men circle her.)

PROVOST STEFANO CECCHI: The punishment is death, girl. Death. Tell us the truth and you will not die. Splenditello or Benedetta?

(BENEDETTA, wrapped in the blanket, stands on the outside of the circle.)

BENEDETTA: *(Softly)* Bartolomea.

(With each of the following lines the men's voices become louder and more demanding. They overlap each other without waiting for the other to finish.)

FATHER PAOLO RICORDATI: Splenditello or Benedetta?

ANTONIO: Splenditello or Benedetta?

PROVOST STEFANO CECCHI: Splenditello or Benedetta?

FATHER PAOLO RICORDATI: Splenditello or Benedetta?

ANTONIO: Splenditello or Benedetta?

BARTOLOMEA: No! Stop! I can't think!

(The increase of loudness and pace of the men should not lessen for BARTOLOMEA's line. They should run their lines right over hers. She needs to fight to be heard.)

PROVOST STEFANO CECCHI: Splenditello or Benedetta?

FATHER PAOLO RICORDATI: Splenditello or Benedetta?

ANTONIO: Splenditello or Benedetta?

FATHER PAOLO RICORDATI: Splenditello or Benedetta?

ANTONIO: Splenditello or Benedetta?

BARTOLOMEA: *(Looking to BENEDETTA)* Forgive me. *(To MEN)* Benedetta.

PROVOST STEFANO CECCHI: You have saved yourself, girl.

(FATHER PAOLO and ANTONIO drag her off. Both women hold their hands toward each other. The PROVOST and BENEDETTA remain facing each other alone on stage. They stare at each other a moment. The PROVOST walks toward her.)

BENEDETTA: *(Sincerely)* I'm sorry you're disappointed. *(The PROVOST slaps her across the face hard. BENEDETTA takes a moment to recover.)* I forgive you. *(The PROVOST slaps her again.)* I forgive you, Monsignor Provost.

(BENEDETTA is affected, but quickly tries to recover. The PROVOST raises a fist and is about to slam it into BENEDETTA's face. Her eyes hold his. He lowers his fist without hitting her. He kisses her hard on the lips as if she were a whore and exits. BENEDETTA, left alone on the stage in blanket and bare feet, looks very vulnerable. She listens to the charges against her and the verdict).

PROVOST STEFANO CECCHI: *(Offstage)* Benedetta Carlini, you have been found guilty of being a false prophet. Your sins are many. You led people to wrong beliefs, demons possessed your body.

FIORA: *(Offstage)* And I saw her cutting the stigmata into her own self.

PROVOST STEFANO CECCHI: *(Off Stage.)* You committed sins against the flesh. According to the writings of St Teresa of Avila, a sister who commits sins against the flesh must be imprisoned for life with no pardon. You will be imprisoned within these convent walls for the remainder of your life. No sister will be permitted to speak to you, or they will experience your same fate. You will have your veil and scapular removed. (*ANTONIO enters and roughly pulls off BENEDETTA's veil. She is either bald or has very short scraggly hair.*) You will only be permitted to leave your chamber for breakfast and to hear morning mass three times a week. You will crawl on the floor behind the other sisters.

(*FIORA enters and pushes BENEDETTA to the floor*)

PROVOST STEFANO CECCHI: You will eat your breakfast near the refectory door so that the other sisters must step over you in their comings and goings.

(*OLD CATERINA, BARTOLOMEA, FIORA and YOUNG NUN enter, wearing shrouds and hoods over their heads. They step over BENEDETTA as they enter. FIORA and the YOUNG NUN, encouraged by FIORA, kick BENEDETTA. The OLD NUNS sit at the table.*)

BARTOLOMEA: I should go to her.

CATERINA: Bartolomea, you have to think of yourself.

FIORA: Yes, you don't want to end up like her, do you?

PROVOST STEFANO CECCHI: *(Off Stage)* Three times a week you will be permitted bread and water as your nourishment.

BARTOLOMEA: I won't talk with her. I'll just bring her this bread.

(*BARTOLOMEA moves slowly as an old woman to BENEDETTA. She bends down to give her the bread. The old woman grabs BARTOLOMEA's sleeve, but this time BARTOLOMEA does not pull her off. They look into each other's eyes.*)

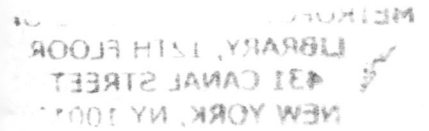

PROVOST STEFANO CECCHI: *(The PROVOST enters, leaning heavily on a cane. He is now in his mid to late seventies and very tired.)* This is the thirty-fifth year of Benedetta's imprisonment. Her story was passed down from parent to child to grandchild. In the year of our Lord, 1631, plague came to Pescia. as Benedetta had warned. Many believed it was God's judgment upon us. Two years later the work of the mathematician, Galileo Galilei, was banned by the Office of the Inquisition securing forevermore the earth's rightful place in the center of the cosmos. Soon Mother Benedetta will die and when she is laid out in the convent the whole town will bang at its doors to be let in. They will want only to touch a bit of the cloth she wore so that they might be blessed, but the church fathers and government officials will send them away.

(The PROVOST exits. BARTOLOMEA leaves the bread for BENEDETTA and returns to the table).

YOUNG NUN: Who is that old woman? What did she do that was so terrible that we should treat her thus?

CATERINA: She ruled the world. That was her crime.

FIORA: Ruled the world? Hah! She was a fool and she made fools of us all.

CATERINA: Mind your tongue. In that time and place so long ago Pescia *was* the world. And *she* held the world in her hands breathless, waiting, hoping. The government stopped, the church feared to confront her. She told us there would be plague and there was. *(Beat)* Sisters. For eight years. Eight glorious years that mere bit of a girl-- ruled the world.

(*As CATERINA says the above speech the lights gradually fade from OLD NUNS and a spotlight comes up on OLD BENEDETTA tearing at the bread with her teeth, animal-like. At the end of the speech the spotlight holds a moment on OLD BENEDETTA and then fades to black.)*

End of play

NOTES